Contents

Archbishop Daniel E. Pilarczyk

'What Must I Do?'

Morality and the Challenge of God's Word

CINCINNATI, OHIO

Scripture citations are taken from *The New American Bible With Revised New Testament*, copyright ©1986 by the Confraternity of Christian Doctrine, and are used by permission. All rights reserved.

Cover and book design by Julie Lonneman

ISBN 0-86716-209-0

Published by St. Anthony Messenger Press
Printed in the U.S.A.

Introduction

Again and again in the New Testament people ask, "What must I do?" or "What must we do?"

Before the ministry of Jesus gets under way, the question was put to John the Baptist (see Luke 3:10ff.). Tax collectors, soldiers and the rest of the populace heard John's preaching and asked him, "What then should we do?" To each group John gave an answer appropriate to their situation: Share with those who do not have, don't collect more than what is prescribed, don't try to get rich on the people around you.

After Jesus had begun to preach, a rich young man came to him and said, "What must I do to gain eternal life?" Jesus tells him to keep the commandments, lists some of them and adds, "...and love your neighbor as yourself." He goes on to invite the man to change his way of life and to "Come, follow me" (see Matthew 19:16-22; Mark 10:17-21; Luke 18:18-23).

On another occasion, a legal scholar asks the same question (see Luke 10:25-28). This time Jesus answers with a question: "What does the law say?" The man answers with citations from the Hebrew Scriptures to the effect that we must love God with our whole heart and love our neighbor as ourselves. Jesus affirms the man's response: "Do this and you will live."

In the Gospel of John the question occurs at the beginning of Jesus' discourse on the bread of life (see John 6:28ff.). The people ask him, "What must we do to accomplish the works of God?" He answers, "Believe in the one God has sent."

People continued to ask this question even after Jesus had finished his earthly ministry. Peter's address to the people on Pentecost is an overview of the significance of the life and death of Jesus. After he finishes, the people ask Peter and the other apostles, "What are we to do, brothers?" Peter answers, "Repent and be baptized in the name of Jesus Christ" (see Acts 2:14-38).

Still later, in Philippi, when Paul and Silas were set free from imprisonment by an earthquake, the terrified jailer asks, "Sirs, what must I do to be saved?" Paul replies, "Believe in the Lord Jesus" (see Acts 16:25-31).

What must I do? What must we do? This question seems to rise spontaneously to the hearts and lips of the men and women of the New Testament who heard the word of God. How am I supposed to respond to what I have heard?

If we were to make a composite and ordered listing of all the answers given to that question in the passages I have just mentioned, the list would probably be something like this: Love God with your whole heart; love yourself appropriately; love your neighbor as you love yourself; do not kill, commit adultery, steal or lie; honor your parents; repent; believe in Christ and follow him; be baptized. This is how God's messengers have answered when people asked what response was expected to the challenge of God's word. This is how God's word answers us when we ask, "What must I do?"

Lots of further questions arise when we ask that basic question and when we consider the answers that Sacred Scripture gives. Why do we have to *do* anything at all? What does it mean to love God and love ourselves and love our neighbor? Why does God command us not to kill or commit adultery or steal or lie? Why should we honor our parents? What does repentance entail? What does it mean to follow Christ and believe in him? Why should we be baptized?

My purpose here is to offer some answers to those questions, to provide some commentary on what Scripture says about what we must do and why. This book will not provide specific answers to every possible question about what we must do, but it will attempt to provide the fundamental framework in which those answers must be sought. We might say that we are exploring the moral implications of responding to the Lord.

From the very beginning the Church has been concerned with *morality*, that is, what we are supposed to do if we would be faithful to what God asks of us. In the past few centuries, this concern has developed into a scholarly specialty known as moral theology. From one point of view, moral theology seems to provide thousands of principles and rules that govern every aspect of human behavior. (The moral theology textbook that I used in the seminary is two big volumes, a total of more than eleven hundred pages, and it deals with everything from fundamental questions such as the nature of human acts to details concerning the operation of pawnshops.) From another point of view, however, moral theology is really a commentary on the answers that God's word gives us to the question, "What must I do?"

It is important for us to understand the purpose of the Church's moral teaching because, if we do not understand it correctly, we will miss its whole point and end up either doing the wrong thing or not really "doing" anything at all.

Sometimes I hear people complain that the Church's teachers seem to have de-emphasized moral teaching over the last ten or twenty years. "When was the last time you heard a priest preaching a moral sermon?" they ask. In a sense they are right. We don't preach about the details of Christian behavior as much as we used to. But we do preach about basic attitudes and basic Christian formation more than we used to. I suspect that here, as in so many other aspects of the Church's life, a redressment of balance is at work. Under the guidance of the Spirit, the Church seems to be tempering a morality of "dos" and "don'ts" with a morality of "whys" and "hows."

Trying to find a new balance does not mean going from one extreme to another. One extreme is called legalism. The legalist doesn't really want to know *why* certain behaviors are called moral or immoral, or how a specific moral action fits into his or her faith life. The legalist just wants to know what the norm is. How much can I shade the truth on my tax return before it really becomes sinful? How late can I come to Mass and still fulfill my Sunday obligation? And, of course, there is the golden oldie that every high school religion teacher heard when teaching about sexual morality: "How far can we go before it's a mortal sin?" From the legalist's point of view, moral behavior means keeping the rules and nothing more; the better you know the rules, the better off you are. It doesn't matter why the law is there, as long as you keep it. Legalists like to have lots of answers, just in case the proper question ever arises.

The other extreme is relativism. For the relativist, it doesn't really matter what you do, as long as you do it for the right reason. It's really all right to get an abortion if your situation is desperate enough. Divorce and remarriage are perfectly appropriate when the commitment I made becomes too burdensome. For the relativist, all norms are merely guidelines to be measured against one's personal dispositions.

Probably the total legalist is as imaginary as the total relativist. But putting the two positions side by side serves to illustrate that each extreme needs to be counterbalanced by the other. The reason we do what we do is as important as what we do. Just doing the right thing isn't enough. On the other hand, there are objective standards for right and wrong, standards against which specific human behavior must be measured. In our complicated modern society, we may not be able to sort out every moral dilemma in advance with total certainty, but that is not to say that there is no place to look for the answers beyond our personal goodwill. Neither goodwill nor rules are enough by themselves.

There is a *what*, a complex of attitudes and behaviors that have a reality beyond individual inclination. There is a *must*, a demand from the Lord implicit in his message of love for us. There is also an *I*, that subjective composite of basic orientation and personal choices that, together, serve to form our personhood and color every aspect of our life. There is a *do*, a series of actions still unrealized, of decisions still to be taken. These elements form the question that was put to John the Baptist and Jesus and the apostles, the question that we each ask ourselves over and over again, the question whose answers will determine the success or failure of our human adventure: "What must I do?"

Questions for Reflection

Do I ever wonder what God wants me to do?

When I hear the word *morality*, what do I think of?

Am I more inclined to legalism or relativism?

Chapter One

To Do and Not to Do

A popular poster some years ago showed a child in ragged clothes standing near a tumbledown shack. The caption was, "God made me. God doesn't make junk."

Another sign that some people hang on their wall says, "Please be patient. God isn't finished with me yet."

These few sentences are filled with wisdom. They provide the foundation for the moral life of the Christian believer, the basis on which we discern what we must do. "God made me." We didn't make ourselves and therefore we don't belong to ourselves.

"God doesn't make junk." We are not throwaway creatures. No matter how tattered our lives seem at times, we are always and ever precious to God.

"God isn't finished with me yet." God made us as creatures who grow and develop. We do not have the fullness of what God meant us to be the instant we are born. God gives that fullness to us a little bit at a time, throughout the course of our lives.

But there is still more. To be sure, we belong to God and we are precious and important to him, and God is still working on us. But God does not choose to work alone. God invites our collaboration to grow into what he had in mind for us to become and to be. The moral life of the believer consists in the way the believer works with God to carry out God's plan for each individual and for the world at large.

We are not our own: This is the basic principle of human life. We do not belong to ourselves. We are therefore not at liberty to deal with ourselves however we want, to treat ourselves any way we wish. We are, as it were, on loan to ourselves from God, and the basic direction of our life has already been determined by its owner. We belong to God and we must treat ourselves as God's, not as our own. All the "rules" of Christian morality, all the "dos" and "don'ts" are reflections and consequences of that basic reality.

Yet in another way we *are* our own. We are not mere passive recipients of what God gives us, but rather coworkers—workers with God in becoming what he has in mind for us to be. In many ways, we are still unfinished, and God calls us to assist in bringing ourselves to completion. For this purpose God gives us the capacity to choose and to do: to choose from the numberless different options that are given us each day; to do one thing rather than another in our task of working together in making us what God intended us to be. To that extent, we are our own.

Human freedom—the capacity to choose and to do—is one of the most fascinating forces in God's world. When God gave us freedom, God gave us the power to have a hand in what we will be. In a way, human freedom is really a share in God's own creative capacity. It empowers us to work with God as cocreators of ourselves. In making us free, God makes us like himself.

God takes our freedom seriously. God doesn't keep us from making bad choices or from harming ourselves or from moving off in counterproductive directions. God wants us to work freely at our task of co-creation, and so he lets us alone even when we are doing a bad job at it. If God were to do otherwise, it would mean that we really aren't free at all, that God was really keeping all the controls in his own hand. Conversely, when we make good choices, when we do right, the choices and the doing are ours and they make a real difference to what we become. What we do is important because God takes us seriously.

We belong to God, yet we are called to work at our own creation by making free choices about what we are to do. That's Christian morality in a nutshell.

Of course, if we are going to work appropriately, we have to have some idea of what God intends for us. God has such great plans for us that even Jesus seems to have found it hard to express them. He uses terms such as *salvation*, *the kingdom* and *eternal life*, terms that have become so worn with usage over the centuries that people sometimes think they don't mean much any more. We might say that God intends us to find fulfillment in all the areas of potential we have been given: understanding and love, the appreciation of beauty, community, self-awareness, gratitude. But Jesus teaches us that salvation, the kingdom, eternal life are even more than just becoming the best self we can possibly be. They also somehow involve becoming like God himself, participating not just in our own individual life but in God's life as well. That's what God has in mind for us. That's the goal that God invites us to pursue.

We cannot achieve any of this for ourselves. The end toward which we work is no more our own accomplishment than is our beginning. It's all God's doing. We cannot make eternal life for ourselves. We cannot earn salvation. We cannot bring ourselves to fulfillment. We can only *respond* to the invitation and the capability that God has given us. That's why we speak of human moral activity as the realm of "response ability." We are called to answer God's invitation, and we are answerable (that is, responsible) for the way we reply. We collaborate in our own creation by the way we respond to the Lord.

All this being the case, it is easy to see that "being good" is not something we do so that God will give us a prize when our life is over, just as "being bad" is not a matter of violating the rules and having God make a penalty call on us. "Being good" means deciding and doing in accord with what we are and what God means us to be. It brings with it an interim fulfillment now, an interim happiness that constitutes a step toward our final fulfillment when God and we will have finished our task of creation. "Being bad" means misusing the gifts that God has given us. It means walking in a direction that does not lead us to where we are meant to be. It means making ourselves unhappy, even now, by doing a kind of violence to what we are and what we are meant to become.

This is not to say, of course, that being good or being bad always bring immediate satisfaction or pain. Sometimes the short term results of being good are very painful and the short term results of being bad are very satisfying. But the direction in which these acts carry us constitute their deepest significance. Even if we are not aware of the results of a specific act in us, the results are there nonetheless. Each and every moral decision contributes to the response that we make to God's invitation to become what he has in mind for us.

Perhaps the greatest danger that people face is the temptation never really to "do" anything at all, to take things as they come, to react according to the whim of the moment, to presume that it's somehow all going to turn out right. Such an attitude implies that God has no real plan for us, that we are not really involved in the pattern of our life, that we bear no responsibility, that our attitudes and behavior don't really make any difference for ourselves, for others or for God. It has been rightly said that not to decide is to decide. To refuse to take moral decisions seriously, to refuse to determine what we must do to respond to God's invitation to work toward our fulfillment is really to reject the whole project. It is to treat ourselves as if we were our own thing, and an unimportant and disposable thing at that. Out of respect for our freedom, God will not force us to "do" if we choose not to, but the emptiness that results will be our doing and not God's.

Ecology, the proper use of the earth, has become an important issue in our contemporary world. Over the past few decades we have become aware that we must treat the ozone layer and the rain forests and all the earth's other resources with responsible respect if we are to live and flourish on our tiny planet. Christian morality is an ecological matter, too. It is concerned with dealing responsibly with the goals and resources that God has given us as human persons so that we can live as his creatures and flourish in accord with his plans.

"What must I do?" we ask the Lord. And the Lord responds, "Respect what you are and respond to what I want you to become. Work with me and we will create something wonderful together."

Questions for Reflection

Why does God find me precious?

What would I like to make of myself?

When am I most conscious of exercising my freedom?

Chapter Two

Loving God: Why and How

When the legal scholar asked Jesus what he had to do in order to inherit eternal life (see Luke 10:25-28), Jesus elicited from him a comprehensive reply: "You must love the Lord your God with all your heart...and your neighbor as yourself." It's all there in a few words. What must I do? You must love.

Love has many shades of meaning. The dictionary defines it as affection based on admiration, benevolence or common interests; as warm attachment, enthusiasm or devotion; as unselfish loyal and benevolent concern for the good of another. Love of God means one thing; love of neighbor means something slightly different; love of music or love of nature something else again. But all the different tonalities of love have basic elements in common. They all imply a positive response to some goodness beyond ourselves. Every sort of healthy love involves a subject (the lover), an object (who or what is loved) and a bond of affirming relationship between the two. One might say that love consists of two "whos" and a "yes."

Consequently when Jesus says that the comprehensive program of what we must do to attain eternal life is to love God, to love ourselves, to love our neighbor, he is calling us to a response, an accepting and affirming response to the goodness that is God, the goodness we find in ourselves, the goodness that is in our neighbor. In this chapter and the next two we will see what each of these loves involves.

Loving God involves, first of all, knowing God because we cannot love what we do not know. Several avenues lead to knowing God. One is the world around us. The fact that anything exists at all tells us that it has a cause. Only nothing comes from nothing, so if something exists, something or someone caused it.

Just as the existence of the world teaches us that there is a cause, so also the nature of what exists teaches us something about that cause. The kind of world we live in reflects the kind of creator that called it into being.

But God wasn't content to let us come to know him just through the world around us. God also took the initiative to tell us about himself, not in some abstract and theoretical way, giving us a philosophy lesson, as it were, but by becoming involved in our world and in our human existence. For example, Scripture describes God walking with Adam and Eve in the garden and speaking to Moses in the burning bush. But that wasn't enough. In Jesus, God became a human being like us. He came into our midst to speak to us in our own human words, to demonstrate in human living not only what human life is supposed to be, but also what God's life is all about. The Church hands on this knowledge about God that Jesus offered us. In the Church, the presence of God in Jesus is extended through word and sacrament.

We can also come to know about God and to know

God through our own human experience. The instinctive sense of rightness and wrongness that we find at the heart of our best self, the unexpected results that we sometimes see from some small act of goodness—this is God's work in us and it provides a source from which we come to know God better than we did before.

It is relatively easy to describe *how* we know God: through creation, through revelation, through personal experience. *What* we know about God from these sources is something else again. Just about everything we know about anything is somehow knowledge about God because the imprint of God is everywhere, from the farthest star in the sky to the deepest and most secret center of our individual personal consciousness.

The vastness and order of the universe, the variety of plants and animals on our own tiny planet, the way things work together, the might of the hurricane and the gentleness of a spring breeze, the endless diversity of human personalities, the beautiful things that human beings can produce in music and painting and words, the depths of evil and of good that men and women are capable of: all that teaches us something about the God who created it. It is no exaggeration to say that the whole world is a theology lesson, a text in which we read about God. But even beyond that, our reflection on creation leads us to an awareness that God is even greater than all this, that even if we could understand everything God has created, we would still not understand God, simply because the Creator is infinitely greater than the creation.

When we turn to revelation, we come upon still further dimensions of God. Through God's words and actions we come to see that he is not an absentee landlord, a creator who did the work and then stepped away from it. Rather, God is involved with the world. God cares what happens to creation, especially about what happens to his human creatures. God watches over them and teaches them and guides them. God lives in the midst of these human creatures not just through the power he exerts over creation, but especially through the divine humanity of Jesus, once present as a historical participant in the world, now with us in other ways. All of this tells us that God sees enough good in us to take a personal interest. This positive response to good is what we have called love. Revelation teaches us that God loves us.

Our own personal experience teaches us still more. The insight that sometimes comes with prayer, the sense of being supported in trial and suffering, the awareness of a meaning in our lives deeper than our superficial activities—all this reassures us that God not only loves *us*, but that God loves *me*.

The only response that makes any sense to all this love is love. As we come to know God, initially through what we are taught about God, then through what we assimilate and learn for ourselves, we become ever more aware of an infinity of goodness, of goodness directed toward us, of goodness that calls for a reply. The reply that God expects is the "yes" of love.

We express our love for God, our affirmative response to the greatness and goodness that is God, first of all by acceptance, by acknowledging God for what he is: the infinite, the creator, the father, the brother, the lover who has loved us first. This acceptance implies submission, an awareness that God is Lord, that God is first and all else is secondary, that our desires and actions have to be brought into harmony with God's loving concern for us, that we belong to God and not to ourselves.

But loving God is not just a matter of mind-set or attitude, nor even just a matter of appropriate behavior. We need to pay personal attention to God, to maintain a conscious awareness of God's presence and activity in our lives. We need to learn to look for the traces of his love and challenge to us in the concrete circumstances of our individual world. To claim that we love God when we never think about God, never deliberately search for God in the fabric of our days, is to love a God who is much too small and too remote to be the real God.

Most specifically we express our response of love to God through prayer. In prayer we consciously address the Lord, in words or gestures or thoughts, alone or in the community of other believers. In prayer we articulate our affirming response to God's goodness. We offer God our submission, the acknowledgment that we are creatures of an all-powerful and all-loving Lord. We express our own sense of unworthiness and limitation. We ask for God's continued care for the goodness that has been entrusted to our responsibility. If we are wise in prayer, we also listen. We express who and what we are by deliberate and conscious attentiveness to the Lord's presence and the Lord's will.

God summarizes all this in the first three commandments of the decalogue: acknowledge me, respect me, worship me.

When Jesus teaches us that we are to love God with our whole heart and our whole soul, he is talking about priorities. He is saying that the relationship between God and us is the foundation on which everything else has to rest. Loving God is not a task that we have to take care of before we turn our attention to other matters. It is the fundamental and all-pervasive call. The response to this call includes everything else that God expects of us. "What must I do?" Jesus could have answered in only two words: "Love God."

Questions for Reflection

Where do I see God most clearly in creation?

Where do I experience God most intensely in my life?

In what specific ways do I express my love for God?

Chapter Three

Loving Ourselves: Why and How

Because God's word tells us that we must love our neighbor as ourselves, we have to understand why and how we are supposed to love ourselves in order to understand why and how we are supposed to love our neighbor.

God calls us to love ourselves because God has made us good and the appropriate response to goodness is love. To say that God made us good is to say, first of all, that God sees our very being as a good thing. Before the question of *what* we are is the fact *that* we are. The basic goodness in us serves as the foundation of everything else. The very fact that we are at all says that each of us is precious to the Lord, that we are important to God, that we are good.

Loving ourselves means responding appropriately to the good thing, the good person that God created in creating us. This involves the realization that we are not our own, but a gift of God given in trust to ourselves. Before we have our first thought, before we carry out our first deliberate action, before we *do* anything, the goodness that God put into us is there.

In addition to the basic goodness of our being,

however, there are also the qualities of our individual personality. God has made each of us to be a one-of-a-kind, unique, irreplaceable human being. No two of us are the same. Each of us is good in his or her own special way. God doesn't produce human beings on a production line. Each of us is an original.

We are good insofar as we are and we are good insofar as we are distinct individuals. We are called to respect and to love this multi-leveled goodness, to respond to it, to develop it.

In other words, in the drama of human existence, we do not play the lead role. God does. Ours is a supporting role, and we have to play it accordingly. That's not to say that our part in our life is unimportant; each of us has a part to play that no one else can carry off. We bear a responsibility for ourselves that nobody else has. When Jesus implies that we must love ourselves "first" so that we can love others, he is suggesting that we can't play our role correctly in the lives of others unless we have the right idea and the right approach to our own part.

Loving ourselves does not mean putting ourselves first and pushing everybody else into second place. Loving ourselves is a matter of respecting what God has made us to be, not of taking on some kind of phony superiority. That's the difference between self-respect and arrogance.

Likewise loving ourselves is not a matter of constantly looking out for our own immediate comfort or satisfaction or profit. Sometimes it involves suffering. Often it requires postponing immediate fulfillment for the sake of something greater or more lasting.

Nor is loving ourselves an affair of ongoing romantic

ecstasy, of just "being in love," any more than loving other people or loving God is. It requires attention and effort. Proper love for ourselves can be hard work.

Loving ourselves has many implications. It involves taking proper care of ourselves physically. It also involves taking care of ourselves spiritually, staying in touch with the Lord so that we will maintain a proper awareness of our worth and not lose sight of our importance in God's sight. Loving ourselves also includes developing God's gifts in us, gifts of affectivity, understanding, creativity and relationship. Education is important in our love for ourselves. It is the way in which we work on the potential that God has put into us, the way we draw it out to maturity and full development. Conscientious use of time is also an element in our love for ourselves. God gives us our life in seconds and minutes, each of which is an opportunity to respond to the goodness in us. When all is said and done, loving ourselves means taking ourselves seriously, even as God takes us seriously.

People sometimes speak of "making something of themselves." "Making something" of ourselves is exactly what loving ourselves involves, provided we are aware that the *self* is not really ours, and that we *make* that self in collaboration with the Lord who has given us the basic material with which we are to work.

We can offend against our love for ourselves in many ways. Suicide is the obvious one. The misuse of our body and our spirit by drug or alcohol abuse is another. Wasting our talents on inconsequentials, or going through life without any real purpose, not having any real idea of what we want to do with the self that God has given us are more subtle offenses. Perhaps the most common offense against our love for ourselves is a lack of authentic self-respect or self-esteem. "I'm not worth much. I'm not very important. I'm not very good at anything. My life doesn't matter much." If all that is true, what is there to love? We can't possibly love what we don't think is any good. And God commands us to love ourselves.

Love for ourselves, then, means respect for what God has made us to be; it means response to what God has given us; it means the wise use and development of the gifts that God has entrusted to us.

But there is more. A paradoxical side to loving ourselves puts the whole enterprise into a stunning new light. Over and over again in the Gospel (some six times in all), we hear Jesus telling us that, if we love our life, we will lose it and, if we lose it for his sake, we will find it (see Matthew 10:39 and 16:25; Mark 8:35; Luke 9:24 and 17:33; John 12:25).

In this enigmatic language Jesus casts the love we are called to have for ourselves into a whole different dimension. He tells us that we are not called to respect and respond to and develop what has been entrusted to us just for God's sake nor just for our own, but for the sake of all God's other human creatures as well. We use God's gifts best when we use them for others. We become our best self when we are least concerned about our individual needs and goals. We love ourselves the most when we are most concerned with reaching out beyond ourselves.

"Losing our life" in this sense does not mean frittering it away in silly things. It does not mean being unconcerned with the good that God has put into us. Rather, it means realizing that God's gifts to us are not just for us but for everybody. It means acknowledging not only that we don't belong to ourselves, not only that we belong to God, but also that somehow we belong to every other human creature that God has created. Our life is not something that God gives us to hold onto or even to work on as a masterpiece for the private enjoyment of God and ourselves. Our life is something that God gives us to share. Loving ourselves is not just a matter of being responsible for what is God's in us. It is also an enterprise of responsibility for the good of all humankind.

God expresses awareness and respect for his own goodness by sharing it with each of us. God loves himself in loving us. He calls us to love and respect ourselves by doing the same, by loving others. Just as loving ourselves is part of loving God, so also loving others is part of loving ourselves.

"What must I do?" I must be involved in a love affair that reaches from the depths of God's being into the depth of my being and out into the being of everyone else who is loved and gifted by God.

Questions for Reflection

What three or four things do I like best about myself?

What plans do I have for "making something" of my life?

What does "giving myself away" mean in my life?

Chapter Four

Loving Our Neighbors: Why, How, Who?

Loving our neighbors is a matter of consistency. If God calls us to acknowledge and respond to the goodness that is himself and invites us to respect and respond to the goodness that is in ourselves, it is only reasonable for God to expect us also to acknowledge and respond to the goodness that is in others. After all, the same goodness, the same participation in the goodness of God constitutes both us and our neighbors. In the last analysis, we are all the same, and if it sometimes seems easier to love and look after ourselves than to love and look after other people, it's only because we know ourselves better than we know them.

Loving our neighbors means the same thing as loving ourselves, that is, to respect what our neighbors are and to collaborate in the development and maturation of what they are called to become.

We might say that loving our neighbors means *willing good* for them. We will good for our neighbors when we affirm the goodness that we see there, when we acknowledge that they have been gifted by God even as we have been, and then offer them our gifts in the development and growth of their own.

If we look on loving our neighbors as willing good for them, we can see how we are able to love someone we don't particularly like. *Liking* has to do with personal resonance. We like people in whom we find common interests and background. We are comfortable with these people. There's nothing wrong with that, of course. But loving is something more. Loving means wanting and doing what is good for the other, whether or not there is a particular association between us, whether or not we find the other particularly attractive. Loving is a matter of wanting and doing. Warm affection is not necessarily involved.

In this context we might point out that our friends are those we both like and love. They are men and women with whom we have found a mutual attraction and for whom we want to do good in a special way. Our friends are those in whom we have discovered the most to love. We want to do the most good for our friends.

Clearly, loving our neighbor is totally foreign to using our neighbor. Using people means paying attention to them for what we can get out of them, for what they can do for us and nothing more. Once we have gotten what we want, they are of no more interest to us. When we use people we treat them like Kleenex—throwaway items whose whole purpose is to make us a little more comfortable. We cannot use people in that way simply because they are not our own to do with as we please. Our neighbor does not belong to us but to God and we have to respect and respond to our neighbor accordingly. Our relationship with our neighbors must have *their* good in mind, not just our own.

Loving our neighbor, then, consists in consciously sharing the goodness and care of God with his human creatures. Loving our neighbor is the practical recognition that God has made us agents of his providence for those around us.

But for which of those around us? Who is my neighbor? After the little dialogue in which Jesus elicited from the legal scholar an answer to the question about what he had to do to attain eternal life, the man asked Jesus this question (see Luke 10:25ff). The scholar apparently expected Jesus to list some criteria of kinship or nationality that would enable him to determine where to draw the line between neighbor and non-neighbor, between those we are called to love and those we are not. Instead, Jesus tells him the parable of the good Samaritan, that wonderful story about the no-good unclean foreigner who comes to the aid of the man who had been mugged, even though the man's own countrymen had passed him by. The point of the story is that being neighbor depends not on religious ties or national relationships but on need. The relationship of being neighbor exists wherever one of us can offer something to another, no matter who we are, no matter who the other is. Jesus' story suggests that if we want to draw lines when we ask who is our neighbor, it should be the circular line of inclusion rather than the straight line of separation.

Jesus teaches us that loving our neighbor means extending ourselves to take care of anyone around us who is in need, whoever the person may be, whatever the need may be. It means offering our concern to anyone who can benefit from it. It means collaborating in God's loving providence as widely as God's providence extends.

What does all this mean in practice? How are we to extend the providence of God to others? How are we to love people we don't know, or people we find unattractive or even repulsive? How are we to love even people who are bad?

One way to approach love for our neighbor is to strive consciously to treat everybody as the most important person in the world. This is not some sort of exercise in fantasy, but an exercise in realism, since everybody is equally important to God.

This involves, as a beginning, looking for the good in others. We can't love what we don't perceive as good, and sometimes the good in others is hard to see. But it is there, and we can find it if we make a point of looking for it. The very fact that another person exists means that God has put good there. It's up to us to find it.

Some people are easy to love because the good in them is so clear to us: people we know well, people like us, people who seem to call forth the best in us. Others are more difficult to love: They are distant from us, they seem to have nothing to offer to anybody, their lives are downright repulsive to us. But they, too, are good. They have a claim on our concern simply because they are, simply because they are God's. One might say that those in the greatest need have the greatest claim on our love because we can will and do the greatest good for them.

One of the reasons people find Mother Teresa of Calcutta so appealing is that she so clearly exemplifies the meaning of love for neighbor. In her concern and care for the poorest of the poor, the nameless beggars dying in the streets, she demonstrates that it is possible to love even those who seem unlovable.

But what about those who are *really* unlovable: bad people, cruel people, selfish and destructive people—the dictator responsible for the deaths of millions, the sex offender who deliberately infects children with AIDS, the embezzler who walks off with the life savings of widows? We are called to love them, too, because God loves them and we are called to be agents of God's love. This kind of love is not easy. Sometimes loving such people, willing and doing good for them, requires an act of faith, a determination to believe that there is worth even where there is no evidence of it.

To say that we are called to love "bad" people does not mean that their wrong behavior is not wrong, or that what people do doesn't make any difference. People do bad things and those things have to be recognized as bad. But there is more to these people than the badness. Something more lies beneath the evil, and we are called to respect and to respond to that something. We are not allowed to write anybody off, not for any reason, because there is something for God to love in every human person, and if there is something for God to love, there is something for us to love, too.

For most of us, loving "bad" people means coming to terms with those who have done wrong to us: the friend who has betrayed us, the spouse who has walked away, the business person who didn't treat us fairly. The loving response is forgiveness—not denying the evil, not saying that it did us no harm, but acknowledging the wrong and deliberately loving the one who did it to us. Forgiveness is a special kind of love. It is "loving in spite of."

Loving our neighbor means being a realist about the way things are. It means acknowledging the goodness of God's good creation and offering our personal contribution toward making it better. It's a lifetime agenda. It's a constantly recurring demand in answer to the question "What must I do?"

Questions for Reflection

What people or what kinds of people do I find easiest to love?

What people or what kinds of people do I find hardest to love?

How do I go about willing and doing good to those who have injured me?

Chapter Five

Thou Shalt Not Kill: Respect Life

So far we have been discussing the general answers that Jesus gave to the question of what we are to do. We have heard him tell us that we must love God, love ourselves, love our neighbor. But Jesus gave more specific answers to the question, too. He cited the commandments. The commandments tell us in greater detail *how* we are to love God, ourselves and our neighbor. Most of the commandments are negative commands ("Thou shalt not..."), but they call for something positive. As we shall see in the next few chapters, the commandments point out special areas and special ways to exercise the respect and response called for in loving God, ourselves and our neighbor.

It's easy to understand why God tells us not to kill. Human life is simply not at our disposal, neither our own life nor that of others. It is God's, a sacred trust that God gives to each of us for his own purposes. We are not the master of our own life or of anyone else's, either in its beginnings or in its conclusion. All human life belongs to God and we have to treat it accordingly.

Even in those extreme circumstances when killing might be justified—in warfare or in capital punishment—

what is morally acceptable is not the taking of another's life but the defense of our own. We may preserve our own life at the cost of another's, but only when our own life is threatened. We are not permitted to go out and kill the enemies of our country at will, any more than we are permitted to execute a criminal just because our primitive instincts seem to tell us that the person who has made others suffer should be made to suffer in return.

It is not just killing that God's command forbids. We are also forbidden to do lesser violence to ourselves and our neighbor, to inflict pain and harm, even if it stops short of the destruction of human life. The reason is the same. Human life is not ours to injure, any more than it is ours to destroy.

We are capable not only of physical harm but also psychological harm to ourselves and to others. We can foster self-contempt. We can inflict on others the violence of verbal abuse or of manipulation for our own purposes. All this is as much an offense against human life as inflicting bodily injury because it involves abusing the precious humanity that belongs to God. Even deliberately fostering anger or hatred in our hearts toward others is wrong because of the contempt it implies for God's good creation.

God's command not to kill, however, is not just a command to avoid certain things. It is a call to positive action, a call to respect and foster and develop what God has entrusted to us. The question that faces us is not just what I must do to avoid harming human life, but also what I must do to promote human life in myself and in others.

Consequently, we have the responsibility to care for

ourselves physically and mentally, to work on the gifts, talents and capabilities that have been given to our charge so that we will grow into what God intends us to be. Our life is too important to God for us to take it for granted, to deal with it casually or without care.

Similarly, it's not enough not to harm those whose lives touch ours. We are also called to assist them in their own project of self-respect and self-development. This may involve things as ordinary as dealing pleasantly and kindly with the people with whom we come into contact or doing simple favors when the occasion arises. It may involve more complicated efforts such as helping people come to grips with sickness or failure, or sharing our resources with them when they are in need, or helping them to take advantage of the opportunities that come into their lives. These are not extras that we can provide for others if we feel like it; rather they are specific ways in which we offer our respect to their human existence.

But God's command not to inflict violence on others, God's call to respect and foster human life, is not just a matter of personal relationships between individuals. It has a corporate dimension, too.

None of us lives alone. None of us lives exclusively in the tiny group of people that we happen to know personally. We are all part of larger groupings: the neighborhood, the city, the nation, the world. In each of these groupings the basic reality is human life, the same human life that is ours, the same human life that we share with our relatives and friends. If we are called to avoid harming our own life or that of those near to us, if we are called to foster and develop the existence that has been given to us and to those around us, we have the same kind of responsibility toward all human life, wherever it may be. The responsibility may be less urgent and its implications less clear, but it is a responsibility nonetheless simply because all humankind shares the same gift of life that we have been called to respect.

Here we enter the realm of social morality, of what we must do not just as solitary women and men, but of what we must do as part of the human community. Before anything else, we need to recall that the society in which we live—whether it be the society of a small town or of our country or of the world at large—is a result of human decisions. Things are the way they are, for good or for bad, because of what human beings have decided to do or not to do. Social structures did not drop down ready made from heaven. They have developed into what they are as a result of the exercise of human freedom. What they will become is also a matter of human freedom and therefore of morality.

Consequently, we all bear some responsibility for what goes on in the societies of which we are a part. We are all called to deal somehow with the violence that is inflicted on human life in this world of ours: the murders and robberies, the wars, the abuse of women and children in families and in employment, the disregard for the health and well-being of the poor, the misuse of resources such as food, air and water. All these (and more) violate God's command not to kill. They constitute an agenda for those who would respect human life.

Likewise, we bear some responsibility for promoting human development. Education, health care, housing, job opportunities, proper provision for people in their old age, personal security in the home and in the workplace—

none of these happen by chance. They depend on the dedication and collaboration of many people working together in the enterprise of respect for human life.

Our collaboration in that enterprise will vary according to our own personal circumstances. Not everybody is equipped to run for public office or to take charge of a soup kitchen or to teach economics in a university. But we are all equipped to be concerned, to raise our voices against violence, to respond to endeavors aimed at making life better for those in need. And because we are equipped and able to participate in some way in the development of our human world, we are responsible for doing so.

We have to deal with many issues in this context of respect for human life in both its individual and its social aspects. There is abortion, which seeks to solve the real human problems of some through the destruction of the life of others. We face the legalization of assisted suicide and euthanasia, both of which imply that human life can be deliberately terminated when it becomes too burdensome or nonproductive in the opinion of the individual involved or of others in society. At the other extreme, there is the tendency to prolong human life indefinitely by technical means even when its natural end is inevitable, as if human life were ours to hold on to as we please, as if continued earthly existence were the only good. In addition to such questions of individual morality, there are the intensely complicated social matters of world ecology, population and food distribution, of educating people to respond wisely to new technologies. These are all life issues. They all require our attention.

But at the heart of it all is God's direction to us about what we must do. We must love. We must love all that God has given us, and the most basic gift of all is the gift of life.

Questions for Reflection

What kinds of violence have I experienced in my life?

For whose life and well-being do I have responsibility?

How do I participate in the social dimensions of respecting and promoting human life?

Chapter Six

Thou Shalt Not Commit Adultery: Respect Relationships

If you ask the average Catholic what the sixth commandment is all about, the answer will be "sex." Well-informed Catholics will be able to tell you that the sixth commandment forbids not only adultery but also fornication, homosexual acts, masturbation, sexual passion outside of marriage, immodest speech and dress, and lots of other things as well.

Such an answer is correct, of course. But the sixth commandment is concerned with much more than sex and sexual behavior. At its roots, the sixth commandment is concerned with human relationships. It deals explicitly with the fundamental human relationship of marriage, but its deepest implications reach into every aspect of serious human association. The sixth commandment is not primarily concerned with sex but with intimacy and faithfulness.

One of the most fascinating aspects of our human reality is our ability to give ourselves away, to put ourselves into second place for the sake of others. We reflected on this a bit when we dealt with the way in which we are called to love ourselves. But this ability to give ourselves away is not just a matter of specific acts, of doing things for other people when we would rather be doing something else for ourselves. God has made us capable of giving ourselves away on a much larger scale than that. God has given us the capacity to give our whole life away to another, to entrust our whole being, down to its deepest levels, to someone else for as long as we live.

This is what happens in marriage. We Catholic Christians believe that when a man and woman marry, they give themselves each to the other totally and forever. Each becomes the most significant person in the world for the other because they have given themselves to their spouse in a manner and to a depth to which they have given themselves to no one else. And the giving is not just for a time, but rather an entrusting of one to the other on a permanent and irrevocable basis. The kind of self-gift that constitutes marriage bears witness to the depths of love God has made human creatures capable of. So much is involved in true marriage that some people think that it is no longer even possible. God's revelation assures us that it is.

This lifelong commitment to another person in marriage is expressed in many ways, one of which is genital sexual activity. Sexual intercourse is the bodily and emotional and spiritual way in which husband and wife speak of their gift of themselves to one another. It is intended to be a statement about the depth of each one's dedication to the other. The importance of this statement in God's eyes is clear from the fact that through sexual activity new human life is generated. God uses this gift of man and woman to each other, this loving dialogue between husband and wife, as the means to provide still further human potential and generosity and self-giving to the world.

That being the case, it is easy to see how sexual activity outside of marriage is wrong. In adultery, that is, sexual activity between two persons of whom at least one is married, a commitment is expressed that the married party is simply not free to make. The married party has already pledged a lifetime, exclusive commitment to someone else, a commitment of the entire person that simply cannot be repeated as long as the original relationship exists. In fornication, that is, sexual activity between two persons who are not married, the action expresses a depth of intimacy and faithfulness that neither party intends. Sexual intercourse is a sign of the total giving of one's very self, permanently and totally, whether one means it to be so or not. To let one's actions say one thing and one's heart and will say another is to lie. It is to be unfaithful to what one is and to the kind of love that God intended between woman and man.

Other kinds of sexual activity outside of marriage are inappropriate because they naturally lead to sexual intercourse, because they trivialize sexual activity or because they foster desires and intentions that are appropriate only between husband and wife.

Some kinds of sexual activity are unacceptable within marriage, too. Sexual activity that is undertaken without love as well as sexual activity that deliberately excludes openness to new human life are wrong because they make this expression of human commitment into something other than it was intended to be, something other than a reflection of God's own love and creativity in human terms. Contraception and unloving sex in marriage are wrong because of what they imply about human intimacy and human commitment.

In our times we have experienced what is known as the sexual revolution. Old taboos have been set aside. Things that were once unmentionable are now discussed openly and in detail in the public media. The sexual revolution has positive aspects in that it has enabled us to deal with this aspect of our humanity in a more forthright fashion than we did before. But it has negative aspects, too. These negative aspects include the epidemic of pregnancies outside of marriage and the spread of sexually transmitted diseases. But perhaps the most devastating effect of the sexual revolution is what it does to human relationships, to faithfulness, to self-giving. To pretend to give one's self in fullness, to signify a commitment when none is really intended, to offer one's self to another only to take back the offering from the very beginning is to trivialize what is deepest and best in what God has made us to be.

The word "adulterate" means to debase, to dilute by the addition of foreign substances. When God tells us not to commit adultery, it means more than not having sexual relations with someone other than our spouse. God is warning us not to water down human relationships through inappropriate sexual activity. God is calling us to respect and foster the full implications of human intimacy and human faithfulness.

There are other kinds of human intimacy and human faithfulness apart from marriage. These, too, must be respected without adulteration.

One such relationship exists between friends. While

the kind of commitment we make to our friends is not the same as that which spouses make to each other, it is a commitment nonetheless. Friendship involves sharing ourselves with our friends—our virtues and our defects, our hopes and our disappointments. Friends share experiences, and one of the joys of a long friendship is the fund of togetherness that friends have acquired over the years. Friends depend on one another for support, advice and tolerance. It has been said that a friend is one with whom you can be together without having to be concerned about what you say. Friends grow together in their humanity thanks to the gifts that each is able to offer to the other.

All this constitutes a special kind of intimacy, a special self-giving that calls for care and attention. Selfishness, indiscretion, insensitivity all undermine the respect that is owed to such a relationship. One can be unfaithful to a friend even as one can be unfaithful to a spouse.

Yet another relationship is the relationship we have with God. What God looks for from us is not the occasional nod, but a lifetime of commitment, of giving ourselves back to the goodness that called us into being, that walks with us each day. It is a relationship that involves the most intimate depths of our being and the widest reaches of our human experience. It involves a faithfulness that engages every aspect of what we are. It is significant that when God's people of the Old Testament turned to other gods, God's prophets used the term *adultery* to describe their behavior.

Sometimes people say that Christian morality is hung up on sex, that it puts an unhealthy emphasis on this one aspect of human life. This is not so. What Christian morality is really concerned about is relationships, about the ways in which we are called to love.

Questions for Reflection

What are the closest human relationships in which I have been involved?

What experiences have I found most painful in my relationships?

What do intimacy and faithfulness mean to me?

Chapter Seven

Thou Shalt Not Steal: Respect Material Goods

We human creatures are a strange combination of spiritual and material. We are capable of loving the infinite unseen God and of entering into lifelong spiritual relationships with other human beings in marriage and friendship. Yet at the same time we are planted deeply in the material. We have material bodies that require our attention. For our very survival we need material things such as air, water, food, shelter and clothing. In order to express ourselves we use physical sounds that constitute words and physical materials such as stone, metal and wood.

Without the basic necessities we die. Without more complex things such as means of transportation and school buildings and libraries, the development of our gifts from God, our creativity and our freedom itself would be mere illusions. We are spiritual beings who necessarily live in the material dimension. We need *things* in order to be what God meant us to be.

It is not enough that these material things exist. They also have to be readily available to us. They have to be *ours* in some way. Unless there is some determination of what is mine and what is not, human life would degenerate into a constant struggle for the satisfaction of immediate needs. There would be little or no incentive for long-term development of the earth's resources. Nobody would really be in charge of anything, and the result would be, at best, a struggle for survival at the lowest levels of human existence.

All this is to say that human society needs some form of private property in order to be fully human. Each individual has to have the right to possess his or her share of the world's goods, a share sufficient to provide for the individual and the individual's family. Private ownership of things is the way in which the material goods of the world are brought into the service of human development. In order for each of us to love God and love ourselves and love our neighbor we each have to have our own portion of what God has made available to us in the realm of the material.

God's command not to steal, therefore, is a command to use material things in accord with their true nature, as means of survival and growth for all human creatures. When God forbids us to take what is not ours, he is not so much concerned with property as with what property involves. "Thou shalt not steal" calls us to respect the person and the freedom of others by respecting what they need in order to be what they are called to be. Stealing is not an offense against property. It is an offense against another person whose property is necessary for personal survival, growth and self-expression.

There are lots of ways to steal. Breaking into somebody's house at night and carrying off the silverware is one way. Embezzling from a bank is another. The woman who puts an extra package of steaks into her purse does it. So does the man who loafs on the job. Human ingenuity keeps coming up with new ways to take what belongs to others. Sometimes the victim of the theft is obvious, as in a purse snatching. Sometimes the victim is a whole group of people, as when an employee steals from a corporation. But in every case, stealing involves taking what belongs to somebody else, misappropriating material things, depriving somebody of what is really an extension of their human person. All stealing is an offense against the dignity of the human person, a violation of the respect that we owe to one another.

But our right to material things is not unlimited. It is not the case that each of us is supposed to get as many things as we can in order to maintain and develop ourselves and our families and that everyone else is simply to keep away from what is ours. If that were so, human existence would degenerate into a gathering of self-serving individuals, each interested only in the self, each intent on warding off the other.

God created the earth and the material goods it contains for the good of the whole human family. Created goods have a universal purpose. Moreover, what is at issue is not mere survival, not just food, clothing and shelter, but other earthly goods as well, goods such as education, employment, the resources to marry and raise a family, opportunities to grow and develop spiritually. All of these are supposed to be for all of us. And this is where respect for material things gets complicated.

If some people, through no fault of their own, do not

have enough to survive on, while other people have more than they will ever be able to use, then something is wrong. If some must work day and night to get their share of the bare necessities, while others have access to all kinds of human goods without having to exert themselves at all, then something is wrong. Somehow God's intention that everybody have a share of what has been created for them is not being respected.

Of course that's the way things are. People go hungry in our own cities, people who cannot find means to earn their living even though they are willing to work. Others have to content themselves with a bare minimum and have no realistic possibility of bettering their human condition. In a larger context, there are whole countries in which practically everybody lives on the edge of subsistence, in which there is no basic medical care, in which people's life expectancy is far below what men and women can look forward to elsewhere. That's the way things are, but that's not the way God intended things to be.

This is not to say that God intends each human being to have his or her mathematical portion of the world's goods and that nobody has the right to have any more than anybody else. There will always be differences in wealth and possessions. There's nothing wrong with inequality. But when some can't even get the basics that are required for fundamental human dignity, then something is radically wrong.

Why are things this way? Sometimes situations of human misery arise from the greed of others. Sometimes they arise from the destruction of created resources through war or natural catastrophes or from the misuse of resources through thoughtless exploitation. Sometimes human misery exists because other people just don't care. Sometimes human misery exists because other people are not aware that anything can be done about it.

And what can be done? The answer to that question involves economics, education, agricultural science, medicine, social welfare plans, organized charity, legislation on labor, taxation and inheritance, and many other elements. Because the situations of human misery and wealth, of the distribution of earthly goods, are so complicated, there are no easy solutions. Persons of goodwill can differ about the appropriateness and effectiveness of anything that is proposed to remedy the inequities. But it is clear that one thing is essential—a shared awareness that a response is called for, that we are all involved in the project of the right use of what God has given to us all.

On an individual level, all of us who ask "What must I do?" must be willing to do what we can. This means personally sharing what we have with those in need, not just because such sharing will alleviate some of the misery of others, but also because such a sharing will keep us conscious of our responsibility for others. That's a minimum. In addition to that, we should maintain some reasonable interest in the proposals of government and other agencies at various levels that aim at dealing with the social inequities of our world. Unless many people are clearly concerned with these matters, nothing much will change.

Most of all, though, we are called to have a clear and practical commitment to what respect for material goods involves. It involves private property, the right to have our share and the right to hold our share unthreatened. It involves respect for the goods of those around us. But it also involves God's plan for all humankind. It is not enough not to be stolen from. It is not enough not to steal. We are called to love, to love as universally and generously as God has loved us.

Questions for Reflection

What role do wealth and possessions play in my life?

Have I ever been stolen from? Have I ever stolen?

How do I express my concern for those who are less well off than I?

Chapter Eight

Thou Shalt Not Bear False Witness: Respect Communication

To bear false witness against our neighbor means to lie under oath, to commit perjury. Probably most people never commit perjury even once in their whole lifetime. Yet the eighth commandment was one of those that Jesus cited when he was asked about what we must (and must not) do to attain eternal life.

This commandment clearly involves more than the relatively rare sin of perjury, even as the other commandments Jesus cited involve more than murder and adultery and theft. Under the heading of perjury this commandment deals with truthfulness, with the way in which human beings are supposed to communicate with one another.

There are lots of ways to communicate. Animals communicate with wordless sounds and movements of their bodies. Their range of communication seems to be quite limited. In the Holy Trinity the divine Persons communicate themselves totally and fully, eternally and effortlessly, in complete understanding and love. Human beings communicate in many different ways: in gestures and looks, in silence and in music. Most of all, human beings communicate in speech.

But why do human beings communicate at all? What's the purpose of the gestures and smiles and words that form such a large part of our lives? Human beings communicate with one another because none of us is complete in ourselves. We all need others if we are to survive, even more if we are to grow and develop into what God meant us to be. And others need us. We signify and respond to these needs through the various vehicles of personal communication available to us, most often through words. Speech is the expression of relationship, of our need for one another.

Sometimes our needs are basic: "I am hungry"; "I am sick." Sometimes we need information: "Can you tell me what time the bus leaves?" Sometimes we merely express our need to be in touch with somebody else: "It's a nice day" or "It's good to see you." Sometimes we express the very deepest need of our personal being, the need to share ourselves: "I love you."

All human communication is a reaching out from one person to another, an acknowledgment that none of us can exist in isolation, that each of us must receive and give to others if we are to be ourselves. One might say, therefore, that human communication, particularly speech, is an expression of what we are, offered in hopes of becoming what we ought to be. If that is the case, then human communication must be true and respectful. It must be an act of love for ourselves, for those with whom we communicate and for God who communicates with and through his human creation.

To tell the truth means to speak in accord with the

way things are. It means to deal honestly with others in our speech, to deal with what is real. If we express ourselves untruthfully, we not only deal wrongly with the subject matter at hand, but also with ourselves and with the person we address. To a greater or less extent, we make sharing ourselves with the other into something that it is not. We undermine relationship, however serious or casual the relationship might be. One might say that lying is a kind of adultery in words.

For example, if I tell my friend that I am late for an appointment because I was stuck in traffic when, in fact, I lingered to see the end of a TV program, the issue is not really lateness. The issue is the relationship between myself and my friend. The issue is what I am willing or unwilling to do without for the sake of being together. The issue is whether or not I think my friend will understand and forgive the inconvenience I have caused. In the final analysis, the issue is who or what I think I am and who or what I think my friend is.

Obviously there are degrees of seriousness when it comes to telling the truth. Lying about being late for a dinner engagement does not constitute radical unfaithfulness in friendship. It may signify only that we are not as totally straightforward about ourselves as we might be. On the other hand, pretending to be deeply concerned about somebody else when we are only interested in what they can do for us is to posit a personal connection that doesn't exist at all. It is to be deeply false about ourselves and deeply false to the other.

In the last analysis, truth and falsehood are not about words or about facts. They are about relationships, and the moral dimension of communication is determined by its connection with our relationships with one another.

Sometimes we are called to tell hard truths: "You drink too much" or "You're not really doing your job." The issue is relationship, when my responsibility for the other is such that I must communicate things that are hard for me to say and hard for the other to hear. To communicate the hard truths implies that I acknowledge that my life is involved with the well-being of the other, and that the other is important enough for me to take pains with. It says something about me and something about the other.

But it is not enough to be truthful. We must also make our communication with respect. This means being aware that what we say carries with it much more than the meaning of the words we use. It carries with it unspoken intimations about ourselves and about the person we address. The truth can be wrong if it says something other than what we mean, or if it expresses what we have no right to inflict on the other.

The insincere compliment, even if it is true, can be a lie about ourselves, and the hard truth, spoken without concern for the other, can be as violent and hate-filled as a gunshot. What counts is not only what is said but what we intend to communicate.

A decision not to communicate says something about relationships, too. Sometimes when we do not communicate with another it means that we have decided that there is nothing in common between us, that we have nothing to offer one another. Spouses who have communication problems in marriage or friends who are no longer on speaking terms generally indicate that the people involved are no longer sharing themselves with one another. In other circumstances, not communicating can be a sign of love and concern. It is not a service to tell our friends the unkind things that others may have said about them, or to burden them with what they are unable to receive.

Communication is not just a matter of speech between individuals. The whole realm of public communication—the media, advertising, politics, diplomacy—presents particular challenges to truth and to respect for the recipient. It is hard to tell the truth objectively when the vehicle is a thirty-second spot on the evening news. It is hard to communicate in a way that can be rightly understood when the audience is several million people. But these challenges do not absolve the communicator from responsibility. A lie is still a lie even if it consists of a half-truth in a newspaper headline. And contempt for the one spoken to is as real in a cynical political promise as it is in a personal insult.

The challenges of public communication do not have easy answers any more than the challenges of the distribution of the world's resources do. Yet the fact remains that people have a right to truth and respect in communication, just as they have a right to their share of the earth's material goods. Perhaps individuals have the same contribution to make in responsible public communication as they do in social justice: at the very least, they can demand that the issues be faced.

We owe ourselves to one another. We pay that debt, in part, by communicating ourselves to the other and by welcoming the communication that the other offers to us. What we say and how we say it are important, but more important is what is expressed in the exchange. What must I do? I must speak, and in speaking I must love.

Questions for Reflection

How generously do I share myself in speech with those around me?

In what circumstances do I expect to speak and be spoken to? When do I find communication in silence?

With what expectations do I read a newspaper or watch TV?

Chapter Nine

Honor Thy Father and Thy Mother: Respect Family

When Jesus responded to the question, "What must I do?" he cited the fourth commandment after the others. As far as I am aware, scholars offer no particular reason why Jesus changed the order of the commandments. He may have seen the commandment to honor father and mother as a kind of summary of the commandments not to kill, commit adultery, steal or lie. Respect for life, for relationship, for the use of material goods and for communication can all be found in the family.

The traditional family involves the relationship of husband and wife, their respect for the life and person of each other and for the life of their children, born and unborn. Maintaining a family requires material well-being and the careful use of material things. At its best, it involves sharing, each member giving and receiving from the others in a process of ongoing communication.

Families have a history that goes beyond the memories of parents and their children to include parents' parents and their parents in turn. Many families have traditions that reflect their corporate experiences and remind the members that all this didn't start just yesterday. Families imply belonging and dependence because no human being can begin to exist or continue to exist as an isolated individual. Families extend to include aunts and uncles and cousins. Not only can we not exist alone, but even fundamental human groupings are not sufficient in themselves.

The family can teach us that our humanity develops gradually, that we need time and a wide context of loving persons in order to grow into what we are meant to be. We need to learn about ourselves, about others and about God, and the first place we do this is usually within the family. It teaches us that others are responsible for us and that we, in turn, are responsible for others. The family is the ordinary context in which we find out about ourselves and our world, in which we come to terms with what is and is not expected of us as human beings. The family should give us our basic orientation about who we are and what we must do.

When God calls us to honor our parents, he calls us to respect and respond to the processes by which our humanity comes into its own. God made us in such a way that we come to be a little at a time, with lots of help from others. "Honor thy father and thy mother" means looking respectfully toward our parents for what they have been called to be in our lives, collaborators with God in the creation of our personhood. Our parents play a significant role in making us what we are. We are called to honor their best efforts in this task.

The obligation to honor our parents doesn't stop when we turn twenty-one. A relationship forged during childhood will continue in adult years, as we turn to parents for advice or share with them our own experiences of adult life. We should be slow to conclude at any age that our parents have nothing more to give us.

When our parents become older and find it difficult to look out for themselves, we can give back to them some of the nurturance and care and attention that they gave to us during the most vulnerable time of our human existence. To honor our parents in old age is to honor the sense of responsibility which they themselves instilled in us.

While there are spontaneous elements in the family relationship, other aspects of growth in family call for acquired skills—attention, forgiveness, conscious demand and response. It is not easy to be a good parent. It is not easy to grow up. Neither can be achieved casually. These tasks require work and always have. But it is necessary work and there is no substitute for it.

I'm not sure whether anybody can prove that it is harder for families to function today than it was in the past, but our times clearly have their own obstacles. Single-parent families are increasingly common. So are the "yours-mine-ours" families in which relationships between children, parents and stepparents become increasingly complicated. The need for two incomes to keep the family going puts stress on family relationships, as does unemployment. A mistaken need for self-fulfillment often arises when people forget that the most important part of their lives is what they give away in love and service to others.

In addition, many elements in our society encourage isolation and detachment: the multiplicity of TVs and radios so that each member can get his or her programs without needing to be with others, the vast array of sports and other activities that seem to keep everybody busy—and away from home—most of the time.

It may be that the greatest need of families in our time is simply the chance to be together. It may be that the most precious resource of today's families is time. The careful sharing of gifts and experience that make the family the basic educator of its members cannot be accomplished if everybody is always on the run. Perhaps today's best parents are those who take pains to see to it that their families come first.

Respect for the family has a societal dimension because a society is only as strong as the families of its members. No nation can prosper if its citizens have not learned what it means to be human, what it means to share, what it means to be together, what it means to give oneself for the good of others. Ideally, family provides the context for learning these essentials. Society cannot teach these things in detail and certainly cannot legislate them. It is possible, though, for a society to provide the kind of economic and social context in which families can prosper. Those who appreciate the importance of families have the responsibility to insist that government provides such a context.

"What must I do?" we ask. There is not always a specific answer to the question. But the principles, approaches and attitudes—about God and ourselves and our neighbor—that can lead us to the proper answer generally come to people through their families. That's why God calls us to honor our father and our mother.

Questions for Reflection

What are the greatest blessings that I have received from my family?

How much time each week does my family spend together and what do we do that fosters family unity and communication when we are together?

What sort of government action would help families function better?

Chapter Ten

Repent

As we consider the various responses given in the New Testament to the question, "What must I do?" it is important to realize that we are not called to do these things in a temporal sequence. It is not the case that first we love God and later love ourselves and then love our neighbor and after that respect life and relationships and material goods and communication and family. All of these responses are tied together. Each involves the others. We do not really love God, for example, if we misuse temporal goods, and we cannot respect family if we do not appropriately love ourselves.

An awareness of this reciprocal involvement is particularly important when it comes to the last three commands we listed in the introduction: Repent, follow Christ, be baptized. None of these makes any real sense without the other two. We cannot even consider one without implying the rest, so their treatment in separate chapters is only for the sake of clarity.

Repentance is a recurrent theme in the New Testament. The term, in various forms, occurs almost sixty times. In addition, the idea appears in other contexts but is expressed in other words. Repentance was at the very center of the preaching of John the Baptist, of Jesus and of the apostles.

The Greek word that we translate as "repentance" also means changing one's mind or purpose or opinion. It suggests having second thoughts. Consequently, repentance involves something more than just being sorry for our sins. Repentance means going in a different direction.

One might say that there are two levels of repentance. One level is the change of direction from nonbelief to belief, from living for ourselves to living for and in Christ, from faithlessness to commitment to the Lord. The other level is the change of direction involved when we become aware that our life in Christ is not all that it should be, when in sorrow for our sins we return to the ways that we have abandoned.

The first level of repentance involves the basic direction of our lives. What is important to us? How do we determine what we should or should not do? Where does the meaning in our lives come from? When the people on Pentecost asked Peter what they were to do, he told them to repent and be baptized in the name of the Lord Jesus (see Acts 2:14-38), that is, to put Christ at the center of their lives, to acknowledge him as the be-all and end-all of their human existence. He invited them to a change of basic direction. He invited them to faith. Jesus issued the same invitation to the rich young man when he invited him to sell his possessions, give to the poor and "Come, follow me" (see Matthew 19:21). It wasn't the financial arrangements that Jesus was primarily interested in but a change in the man's fundamental value system. He was calling him to faith, to a change of direction, to repentance.

We will see more of this fundamental change of direction in the next chapter, but two things need to be pointed out here.

First, the basic change of direction that is involved with accepting Christ necessarily includes turning away from personal sins. When we give ourselves to Christ, we can no longer live as we did before. Faith includes sorrow for what we were in the past and a determination to live differently in the future. Otherwise accepting Christ in faith really doesn't mean anything.

Second, the basic repentance involved in faith is not a once and for all decision that we make and then don't have to bother with any more. On the contrary, it is a decision that we have to keep working at our whole life long, not because Christ doesn't respond fully to us, but because he calls us to ever deeper association with him. Faith in Christ is not a bus ticket that we either have or don't have, but a relationship that is supposed to grow and develop as our earthly existence runs its course. In addition to that, we have an inherited inclination to sinfulness. If we are not attentive to our gift of ourselves to Christ in faith, if we take it for granted as we turn to other things, we will find that the relationship weakens and can even break off completely, not because Christ has walked away from us, but because we have gradually walked away from him. We need to watch and reaffirm the basic direction of our life because of who and what Christ is and because of who and what we are.

This brings us to the second level of repentance, sorrow for our sins. We all know a lot about sin. One might say that each of us is an expert in it, thanks to the religious formation we have received, but, even more, thanks to our own personal experience. We know that there are little sins and big sins. We know that there are sins against God, against ourselves, against our neighbor. We know that we can sin by desire as much as we can sin by act or omission. As we mature, we become increasingly aware that practically every sin has effects outside ourselves and that therefore sin is rarely, if ever, strictly private.

Sin is a matter of specific desires or acts or omissions in specific circumstances of time and place. But sin can also be more generalized. Earlier in our series we spoke of the call to do, to take joint responsibility with God for what we were meant to be. To float through our lives without proper concern for what God calls us to is to abdicate the very foundation of personhood, even if there is no particular consciousness of specific sins. "I haven't done anything" is not necessarily a claim to virtue.

Repentance means turning away from our sins. It includes an acknowledgment of what we have done or not done. Generalized acknowledgment of "being bad" is not enough because we can't be sorry for what we are not aware of. Repentance includes a determination to do differently in the future, to take a better hold on our lives so as to respond more deeply to God's plans for us. Finally, it includes an explicit expression of sorrow. It means saying to God and to ourselves and to the Church (generally in the sacrament of reconciliation), "I have done wrong and I am sorry and I'm going to try not to do the same again."

Implicit in all this is a renewed sense of direction in our lives. The facts of our sinfulness are important, but the real meaning of repentance does not lie in getting the details right and being able to say them, but in turning our lives around. After all, our lives are not a series of unconnected occurrences, good or bad, but an ongoing story that God and we are working on together. Repentance means looking at the general direction of the story and determining how that direction needs to be changed in view of what we have or have not done.

One of the most significant facets of the reformed rite of the Sacrament of Reconciliation is what the Church asks the penitent to tell the priest. The penitent must tell all serious sins, and whatever smaller sins seem most significant, but the penitent is also called to give some account of the general direction of his or her life. This suggests that, while the details are important, particularly if it is a matter of serious sins, their importance lies in their relationship to the general context and direction of the life of faith in which the penitent is engaged.

Repentance is an integral, constant element of Christian life. All the commands that God has given us are commands to love. All sin, great or small, is a refusal to love—to love God, to love ourselves, to love our neighbor. When we repent of our sinfulness, when we sharpen and renew our fundamental faith commitment to the Lord, we express our willingness to love again, to love better.

God calls us to continual repentance, not because he wants to afflict us with ongoing guilt feelings, but because he wants us to be aware that we have never loved well enough or generously enough or intensely enough to respond to the love with which he loved us first and loves us now. We are in continual need of alterations, of redirection in our lives.

"What must I do?" we ask. And God answers, "Love and repent."

Questions for Reflection

What is the basic direction of my life?

What things am I most sorry for in my life? Why?

How has the Church's sacrament of reconciliation helped me in my journey?

Chapter Eleven

'Follow Me'

Jesus' final word to the rich young man who asked what he had to do in order to gain eternal life was, "Follow me" (Matthew 19:22). On another occasion, when the crowds asked him what they should do to accomplish the works of God, Jesus answered, "Believe in the one God has sent" (John 6:29). In the midst of the earthquake at Philippi Paul tells the jailer: "Believe in the Lord Jesus and you and your household will be saved" (Acts 16:31).

What does it mean to be a disciple of Jesus, to follow him, to believe in him? Following Jesus is not just a matter of doing certain things, of behaving as Jesus behaved. Believing in Jesus is not just a matter of accepting what he taught or of giving assent to a series of propositions about him. Much more than that is involved in following Christ and believing in him. Christian discipleship involves giving and receiving and becoming at the deepest levels of our human personhood.

Following Jesus and believing in him means *giving* ourselves to him in love. For the true disciple, love for Christ is the most important thing in life, it is the fundamental relationship that colors and determines every other relationship as well as every word and thought and action. This is what Jesus called for from the rich young man when he invited him to leave everything and become a disciple. It was not that having things was wrong or that Jesus insisted that everyone who was with him had to have some sort of vow of poverty, but rather that relating to him and being with him was to be the central reality of the follower's life and everything else was to be secondary to that. Jesus calls for the same thing from his followers today.

Being a Christian believer cannot be just one more thing in our lives along with other loyalties, political, national or interpersonal. Responding to the will of Christ as he has made it known to us is the most important thing we must do. Following the teaching of Jesus can be subordinate to no other demand, to no other responsibility. As disciples, our love for Christ has to be the central love of our lives that determines how we are to love everything and everybody else, including ourselves. Christian believers are called to be selfless lovers who give themselves completely and without reservation to the beloved who is Christ.

This is not always easy, of course. There is a cost to discipleship. It involves putting ourselves second. It involves having different goals and ideals from those of people who are not followers of Christ. Material goods and human relationships mean something different to the believer than they mean to the world at large. Self-sacrifice is the norm rather than the exception in the life of the believer because the One the believer follows is the model of self-giving *par excellence*.

But discipleship is not just a matter of giving. It also involves *receiving*. To those who respond to his call to discipleship Jesus gives himself. The same unreserved gift of self that Jesus calls for is what he gives in return. What he gives, however, is different from what we give to him. Jesus gives us not just his affection, not just dedication and concern and loyalty, not just the central place in his attention. Because he is God Jesus can give us more than that. Jesus gives his very self to share in our human existence.

The technical term for God's gift of himself to us in Christ is grace. It is also called justification, divinization, regeneration, divine adoption, re-creation, supernatural life, righteousness, holiness. The reality is so astounding that a single word seems incapable of expressing its fullness. No matter how many words we use, though, it almost seems too good to be true. Yet it is true.

The believer lives not just one life but two—the individual human existence we each receive at birth, but also the life of Christ, the human being who is God.

To say that the believer lives the life of Christ does not mean that Christ stops being who and what he is and that we stop being who and what we are and that some sort of amalgam occurs that is different from each of its components. No, Christ remains Christ and we remain ourselves, yet we are different because of the penetration of our life by his. We are no longer *just* ourselves who live, but men and women who live in and with Christ. His life is extended through ours.

This sharing in the life of Christ is not something that believers are called to keep separate and distinct from their own individual lives, something held apart in special reverence. Rather, the life of Christ becomes the whole rationale for being and doing in the life of the believer. It is supposed to control and determine our whole existence. Our life becomes his, just as his became ours.

Consequently, we must conduct ourselves according to the will and the teaching and the example of Christ, not just because we love him, not just because we believe in and accept his teachings, but because he himself asks us to express him in our lives. Discipleship does not mean carrying out a series of commands about what we must do, but rather carrying out the life of Jesus himself in our individual existence.

It's almost as if Jesus could not content himself with living a single human life in one place for a determined number of years. He wanted to be part of this world of ours everywhere, in every time. So he gives himself to his disciples to bring him to places and times that his contemporaries in first-century Galilee and Judea could not even imagine.

We are not expected to imitate the life of Jesus in its concrete historical details, living the life of a religious teacher in the first century. We are rather called to live as men and women of our own times, in touch with what is going on, part of the action of our world precisely because in that way we bring Christ into touch with the world and the time in which we live. It is not that we reproduce Christ, but rather that we complete his historical reality through our own. We are to bring to realization all that which Jesus, in his restricted earthly existence, could not express.

Discipleship, then, has to do with giving—giving ourselves to Christ—and with receiving—receiving the life of Christ into our own. But discipleship also has to do with *becoming*.

The gift of ourselves is not made once and for all. We mentioned this earlier in the context of repentance. We are creatures of time. We keep changing. What we were at sixteen we are not at sixty. New aspects of our lives call for our attention, we have new elements to offer to the Lord along with our basic commitment to him. Our discipleship has to develop.

Something similar is true from Christ's direction. Christ cannot give us all at once everything he wants us to have and to be simply because we are not capable of receiving it. Even though his basic gift of himself remains the same, the meaning of his life in a senior citizen is different than its meaning in a teenager. The specifics of Christ's self-gift to us develop as we ourselves develop.

All discipleship, therefore, is a matter of becoming. But there is a further dimension to the developmental side of following Christ. None of us can ever say that we have responded fully to Christ's love for us at any stage of our lives. There is always more to it than we have been willing to receive. Moreover, we are selfish and sinful creatures who find it hard to let go of ourselves; we keep discovering pieces of ourselves that we have been hanging on to despite our fundamental decision to give ourselves to Christ. A wise man once wrote that the most arrogant thing a believer can say is, "I am a follower of Christ." At most, and with great diffidence, we may be able to claim that we are trying to become a follower of Christ.

As we consider discipleship, following Christ and believing in him, it becomes clear that the basic question of our lives is not really, "What must I do?" nor even,

"What must I be?" but rather "Who must I be?" And the answer is, "Christ the Lord, God become human, whose life has become my life."

Questions for Reflection

What does it mean to me to believe in Christ?

In what ways is my life different because I am trying to be a follower of Jesus?

What development have I seen in my discipleship over the last few years?

Chapter Twelve

Be Baptized

It all comes together in baptism. When we are baptized we express our basic orientation toward the Lord, a change of direction from nonbelief to faith. We give ourselves to the Lord and begin our journey of discipleship. And the Lord gives himself to us. He begins to live his life through ours. Repentance, discipleship and grace are all tied together in the sacramental bath that washes away our sins and makes us God's son or daughter. When an adult is baptized, these various elements are deliberately expressed and consciously received by the one who receives the sacrament. When a child is baptized, the life of God begins in the child but dedication to Christ and commitment to discipleship are expressed for the child by others and then personally assimilated as the child grows to maturity.

It is clear that being baptized is one of the things we must do if we are to gain eternal life. Jesus told Nicodemus that a person who is not born through water and the Holy Spirit cannot enter the kingdom of God (see John 3:5). His last instructions to his followers before he ended his earthly life were to make disciples of all nations and to baptize them in the name of Father, Son and Holy

Spirit (see Matthew 28:19). In the Pentecost discourse Peter tells the people they must do that; they must all be baptized (see Acts 2:38).

Christ chose baptism as the ordinary means to enter into a special and personal relationship with individual human beings. Conscious and deliberate refusal of the sacramental sign constitutes a refusal of the relationship.

Baptism, however, is not some sort of arbitrary requirement that Jesus thought up as one more thing we have to do. The symbolism of cleansing and the nature of water as source of life and energy express and bring about what happens to us when we repent and begin to follow Christ. In addition, discipleship is not a hidden and private affair between Christ and the believer but a public commitment that calls for a public and visible event to mark its official beginning. Finally, the fact that baptism is something that is done to us, something we receive, signifies that repentance and discipleship and life in the Lord are not our own achievements but gifts of God. We cannot bring all this about on our own. We can only respond to the initiative of God and accept what God means to give us through the instrumentality that God has chosen.

But baptism is more than repentance, discipleship and grace. Baptism also makes us one with God's people. It makes us members of the Church. This dimension of baptism is not something added on as an afterthought, but part of the very heart of the meaning of the sacrament. Just as there can be no authentic repentance that does not involve following Christ, so also there can be no authentic discipleship that does not involve the Church.

God knows us and loves us as individuals. In Christ,

God wishes to enter our personal human existence. But God also relates to us through other people and asks us to relate to him through others as well. We have already seen how this is the case with our natural life and how family is the context in which we grow into the fullness of our personhood. We need the Church for the same reason that we need our natural families: in order to be and become what God intends us to be.

In the context of the Church we come to know the fullness of the truth about God's love for us because the Church is the authorized voice of God's revelation. Jesus has guaranteed that it will never present as his word that which is erroneous. The Church gives us the Scriptures, the written account of God's relationship with humanity. The Church teaches us the implications of that story for our own existence. It teaches us what we must do in order to have eternal life.

But the Church does not just teach and guide. The Church also offers us the fullness of Jesus' life in the sacraments. Beginning with baptism, through which we come alive in the life of Christ, the Church offers us the love and the action of Christ for every stage of our personal journey of faith. Christ nourishes us in the Eucharist, forgives us in the Sacrament of Reconciliation, strengthens us when we are sick. Christ becomes a participant in the married life of his faithful through the Sacrament of Matrimony.

The prayer life of the Church is a kind of extension of the sacraments, the gathering of the faithful to praise and thank the Lord, to express sorrow for our deficiencies, to turn to him for help. In all this, Christ is present and active in his Church.

We need the sacraments and prayer because we cannot become what Christ calls us to be without them. But we also need the other members of the Church. We learn about Christ from the word and example of other believers. No solitary individual can grasp or express the full meaning of Christ's life in us. We need the unique manifestations that come to us through the faith of others. We also need the encouragement of others. We pray better when we see others praying, too. We are more eager to carry out the Lord's commands about what we must do when we have the example of others struggling to remain faithful to his word. None of us can be the Christ we are called to be without the Christ who is in others. And the other members of the Church cannot be who they are called to be without the gifts from Christ that come to them through us.

The Church is not a kind of club to which we belong for the benefits it confers, or a shopping center to which we come when we need something and where we are free to pick and choose among a wide selection of offerings. The Church is the family of those who follow Christ, a family to which we must necessarily belong if our commitment to him is authentic. It is the context in which we meet Christ, a Christ we must accept on his terms and not our own. It is the gathering of the faithful in which we not only receive but are also expected to give.

Being in the Church is not always easy, any more than repentance or discipleship is easy, any more than being in a human family is easy. For one thing, the Church makes demands on us, Christ's demands. Sometimes we would just as soon not be reminded of all that Christ expects of us, but the Church continues to proclaim his will anyhow.

Sometimes what the Church tells us we must do seems excessive, too unrealistic for our day-to-day world. But we must still listen. We must do our best to respond to what the Church teaches because the Church teaches for Christ.

Sometimes being in the Church is not easy because there seem to be so many rules and regulations. We would like to be free just to follow Christ without all the paraphernalia of law. We tend to forget that every community needs some regulation just because it is a community. People need direction when they are together in order to be able to remain together in peace. In addition, many of the rules and laws are really conclusions and applications of the teaching of the Lord; their force comes not from some legislator in Rome but from the will of Christ. To demand that the "rules" be changed is tantamount to asking that Christ teach something different.

Sometimes it is hard to be in the Church because of its other members, limited and weak and sinful people. It would be much easier if the Church's members were all shining examples of what they say they believe and if the Church's leaders obviously practiced everything they preach. But God isn't finished with them yet. The love of Christ is still at work forming and developing his followers to be what he wants them to be. God isn't finished with the Church yet, either. Just as there is history and growth in human families, so there is in the Church. The Church always remains the voice and the instrument of Christ, but the Church is always in the process of becoming a better voice and a more effective instrument. Of course, if the Church were a community of perfect people and were everything Christ ever meant it to be, there wouldn't be room for us, because we ourselves are imperfect and still unfinished.

"What must I do?" we ask. And Jesus answers, "Repent, become my disciple, be baptized, be my Church."

Questions for Reflection

For what am I most grateful to the Church?

What do I find most difficult in the Church?

In what ways is the Church enriched by my being a member?

Chapter Thirteen

Unprofitable Servants—Beloved Friends

The Irish have a phrase that pops up often in their conversation: "At the end of the day." The phrase does not refer so much to the setting of the sun as to any significant conclusion: "At the end of the day we will still have to come to grips with unemployment in our country"; "At the end of the day there will have to be some change in the relationship between Northern Ireland and the Republic."

We have been reflecting together about what we must do, about what God expects of us, about what is involved in our response to God's invitation to be part of his Kingdom. In this concluding chapter it might be helpful to talk about the end of the day, about what we can look forward to when we have come to the conclusion of our doing, when we stand before the Lord with what we have done.

We certainly will not be able to claim to have made a full or even an adequate response to what God has told us we must do. Sin and selfishness are too strong in us, the sin and selfishness we have inherited with our common humanity and the sin and selfishness we have acquired by our own doing.

"Nobody's perfect," we tell ourselves, and we are absolutely right. Thanks to the flawed humanity we started with, thanks to the misuse we have made of that humanity, we are all imperfect: imperfect lovers of God, of ourselves and of our neighbor; imperfect in our repentance; imperfect in our discipleship; imperfect in our participation in the community of the Church. We are all, as it were, flawed merchandise. We are all seconds.

But that's not all. Jesus tells his disciples, "When you have done all you have been commanded, say, 'We are unprofitable servants; we have done what we were obliged to do' " (Luke 17:10). Even if we have responded perfectly to what we must do, we are still inadequate.

The point here is not that the Lord is a master who is never satisfied, no matter how much we do for him, but rather that *we* really never *do* anything for him at all. Everything is God's gift: our life, our talents, the opportunities we are given in our personal history, our family, our friends, our greatest and our smallest achievements, the capacity to *do* at all. All is the free gift of God that we can do nothing to deserve. Even our ability to thank God for his gifts is itself a gift. All we can do is to respond to God's generosity. God's generosity to us is so great that even the best of us can only respond to it in part. God never gets back from us as much as we have been given. We are all unprofitable servants.

This is a hard saying because it implies dependence and none of us likes to be dependent. We prefer to stand on our own feet and make our own way without owing anything to anybody. And that is precisely how things *cannot* be between ourselves and God. To try to make them that way is either to claim for ourselves strengths and abilities that we simply do not have or to reduce the generosity of God to insultingly tiny proportions.

It is here that God's mercy comes into play. Mercy means compassionate treatment to those in misery or distress. It means forbearance in exacting what is one's due. And our God of mercy knew what was involved in creating us. God knew that we would become self-seeking and shortsighted and sinful, that we would never be able to make an appropriate response to what we would be given. But God created all of us anyway and cared for us and loved us and even became one of us in Jesus. And what God did for all of us, God continues to do for each of us, not because of anything he can gain from us but just because he is a God of love and of mercy.

We do not need to earn our salvation. In fact, salvation is something we cannot earn. It is something that God gives us in his mercy. Gaining eternal life is not a matter of fulfilling certain requirements, but rather of accepting what a loving Lord wants to confer on unprofitable servants.

But the Lord does not think of us just as unprofitable servants. He also looks on us as his friends. At the Last Supper Jesus told his disciples, "You are my friends if you do what I command you" (John 15:14). Here is a whole new relationship, different from that of master and servant. Friends are those who share themselves with one another. Friendship is not a matter of just doing what one is told, but of responding to the desire of a friend out of an awareness of its context, out of knowledge of what a friend has in the depth of his heart. And what Jesus had

—and has—in the depth of his heart was love, love for the Father, love for his disciples, love for us.

Doing what he commands us is not a matter of carrying out some itemized agenda, some list of errands that we are given and that must be finished up by a certain time. That's the mentality of a servant. Doing what Jesus commands is rather a matter of relationship, a loving relationship between friends, a loving relationship with him. We can never finish what we must do, because what we must do is to love him and to love one another in response to his love for us. Friendship is not a task but a process, a process that is never concluded until the friends have no more of themselves to give each other.

This is where hope comes into the picture. Hope is the realistic expectation of something good, and Jesus is never finished offering good to us. No matter how much we have already received from him—including his life in our own life—Jesus always has more to offer us: more love, more forgiveness, more concern and, yes, more challenge. We never really finish responding to him because he never finishes addressing us. It is therefore always realistic to expect something good from the Lord because he is the Lord of mercy and love. It is always right to hope in the Lord because he is the Lord and because he is our friend.

As I was beginning this book, I was discussing the ideas with some colleagues of mine. I asked them what one could point to as the specific difference in the life of a Christian believer as opposed to the life of a reflective and naturally virtuous atheist. Would there be any difference in external behavior? Could you tell believers from nonbelievers just by the way they speak and act?

I'm not sure we came to any definitive conclusion, but we did agree that the underlying attitude of the Christian's life would be different because it would be founded on hope, the hope that comes from the friendship of Christ. Maybe believers smile more.

When all is said and done, what must I do? I must accept the gifts of the Lord and I must respond to them in all the ways that God has made clear: doing some things, not doing others, respecting what God is and what I am, giving myself to Christ and receiving Christ in return, loving and being loved, mindful that God reaches out to all my sisters and brothers even as God reaches out to me. At the end of the day, I must stand in hope before the mercy and the love of the Lord, as an unprofitable servant, to be sure, but also as a beloved friend.

Questions for Reflection

Is there any sense in which I am a profitable servant of the Lord?

What does friendship with Christ mean for me?

Am I a hopeful person? Why? Why not?

What must I do that I am not already doing?